The Bus

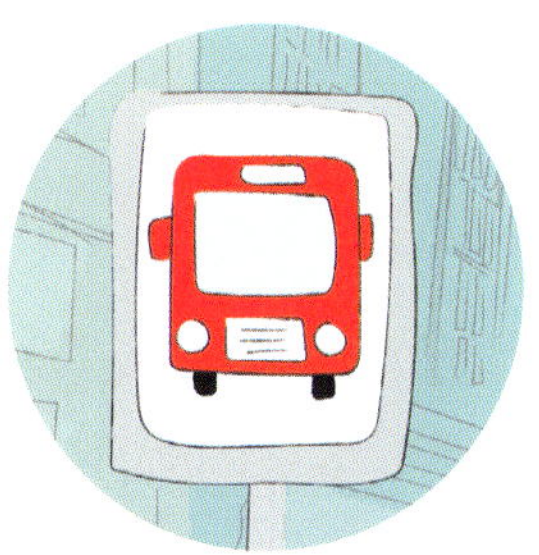

Written by
Stephen Rickard

Illustrated by
Michelle Breen

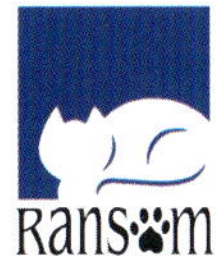

Ransom

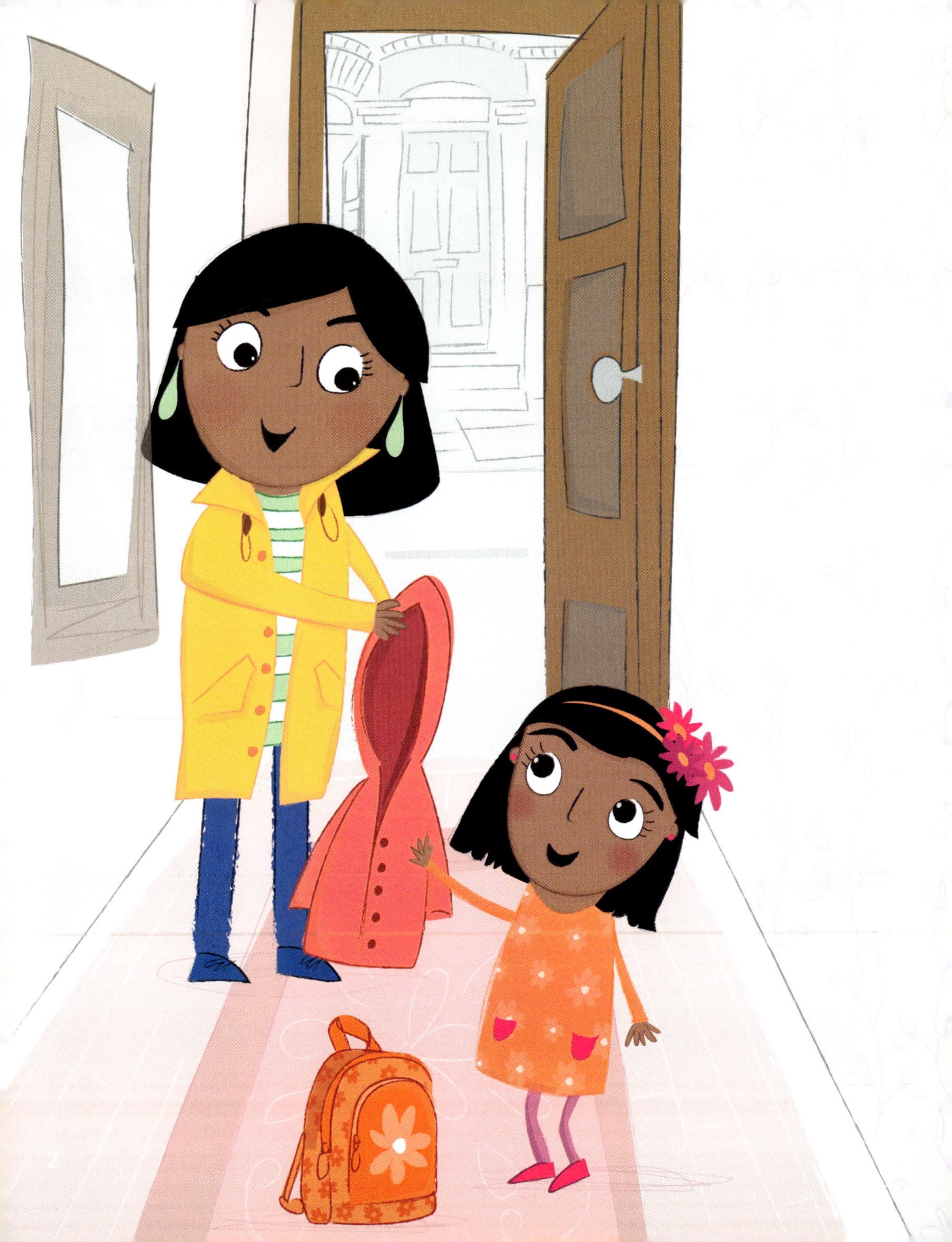

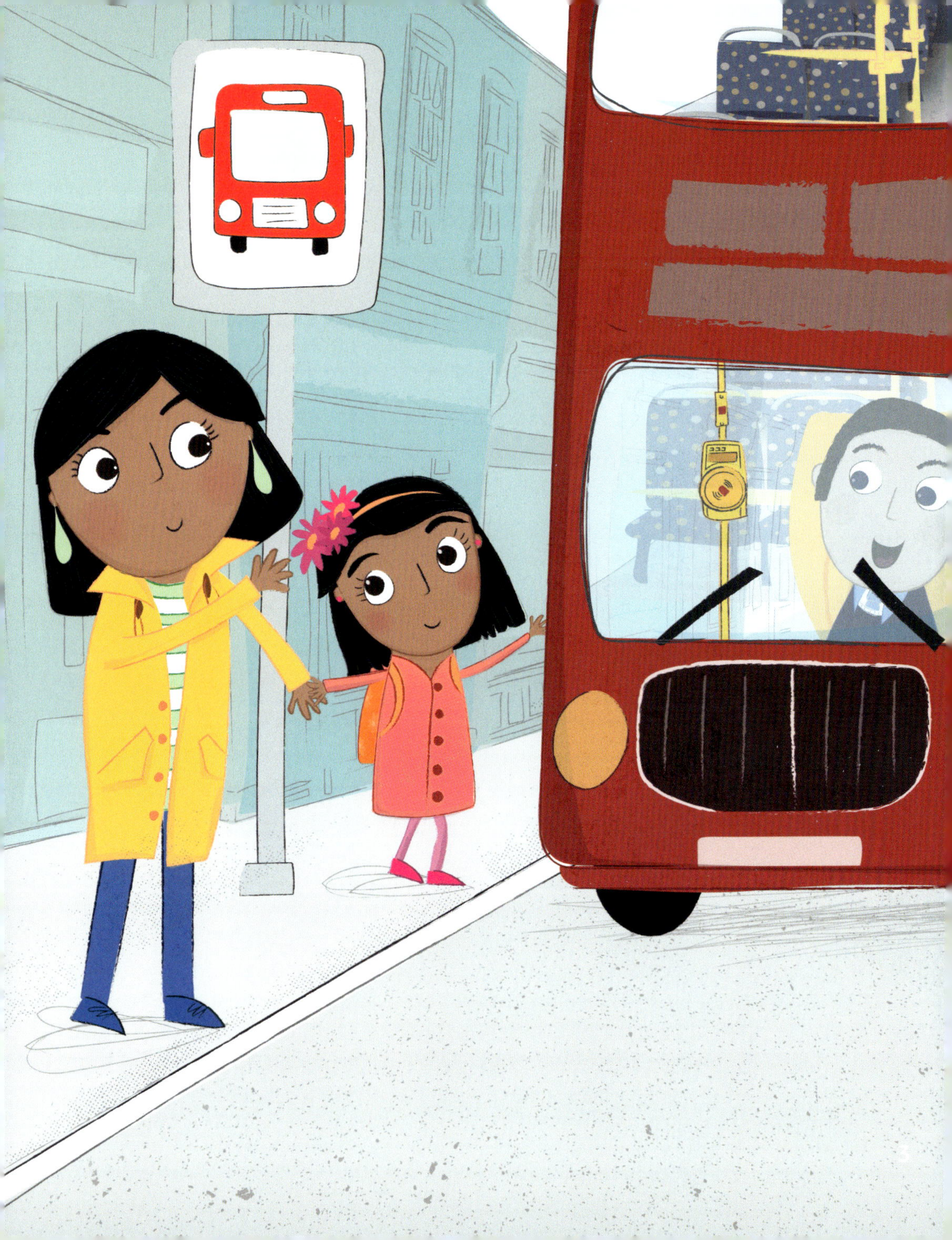

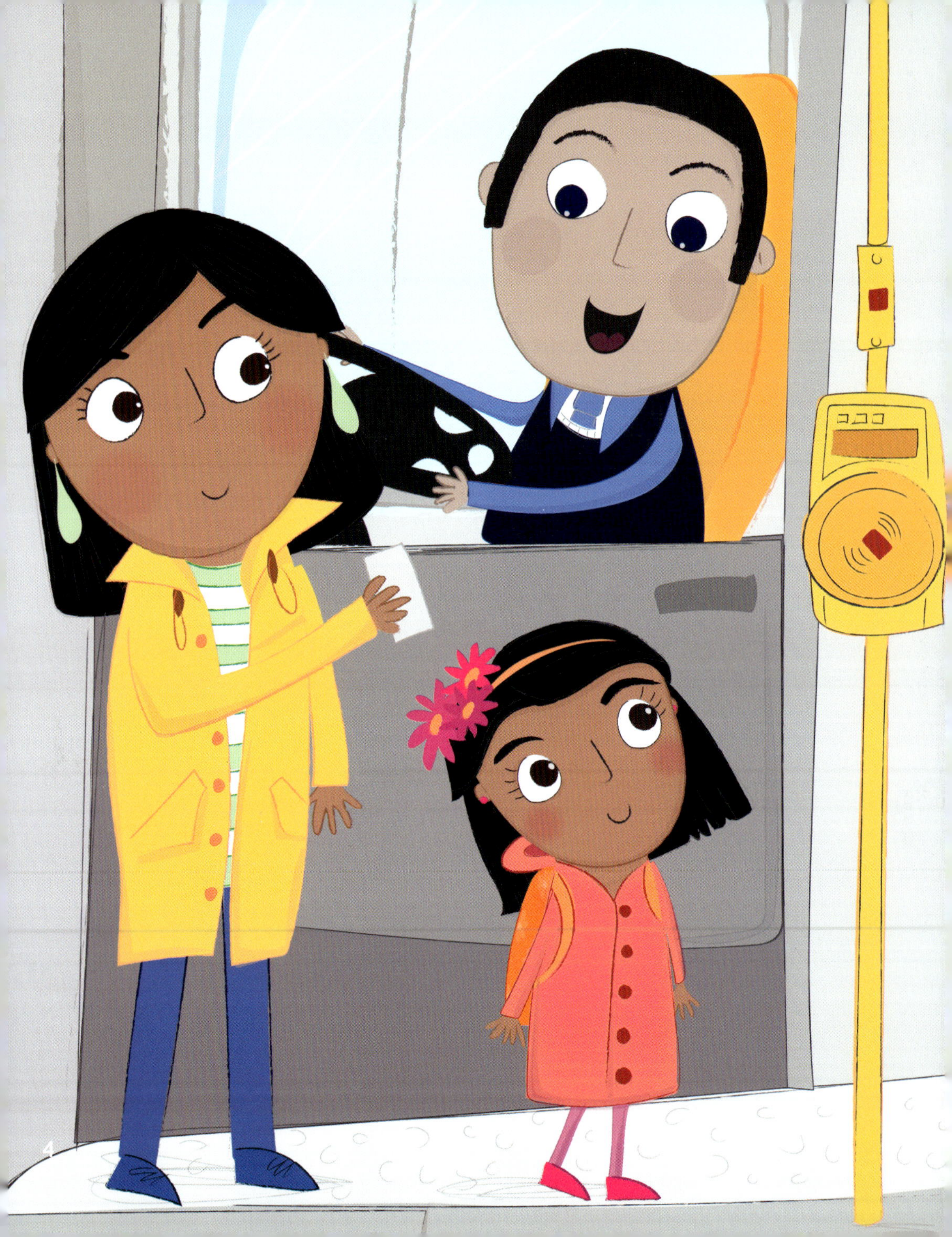

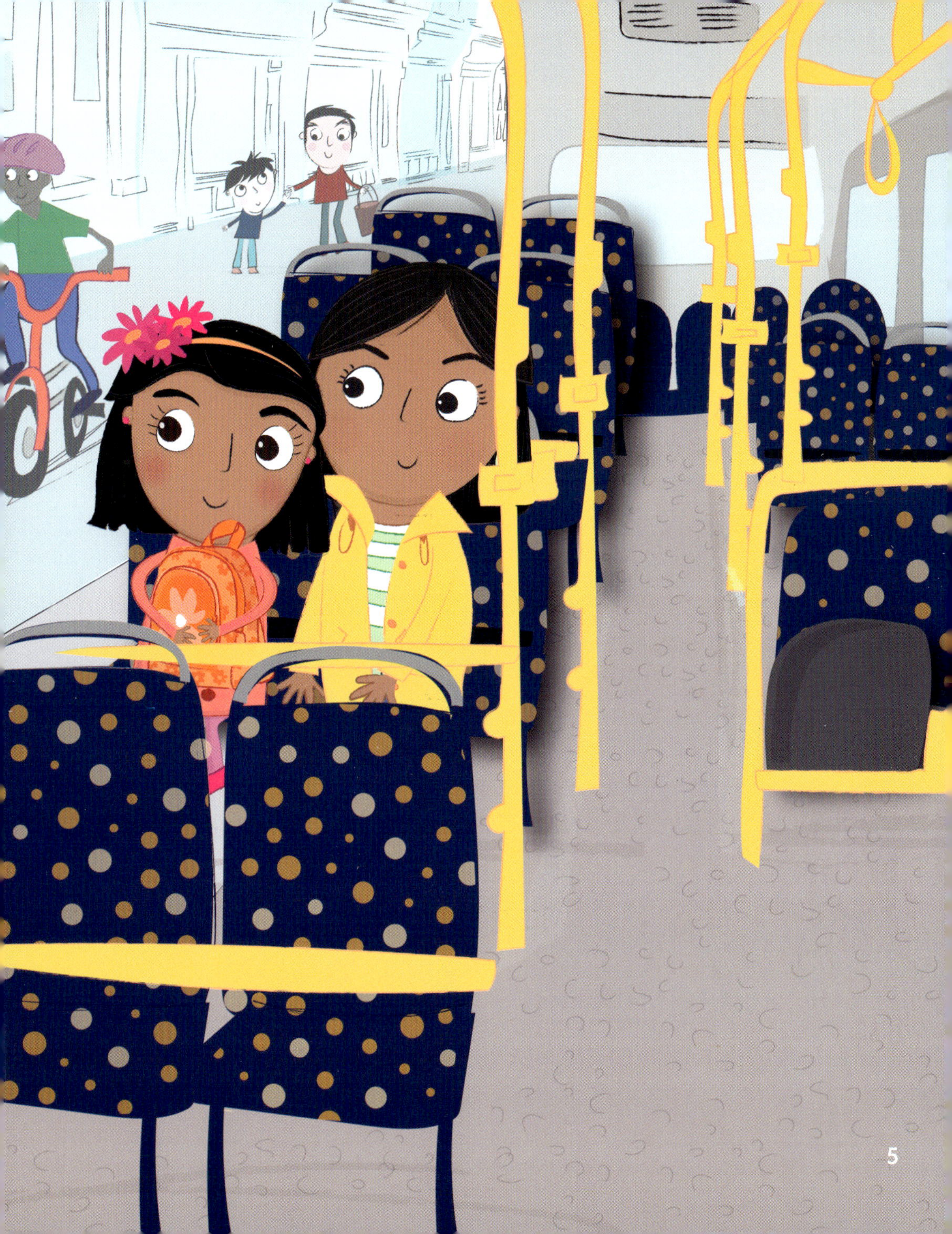

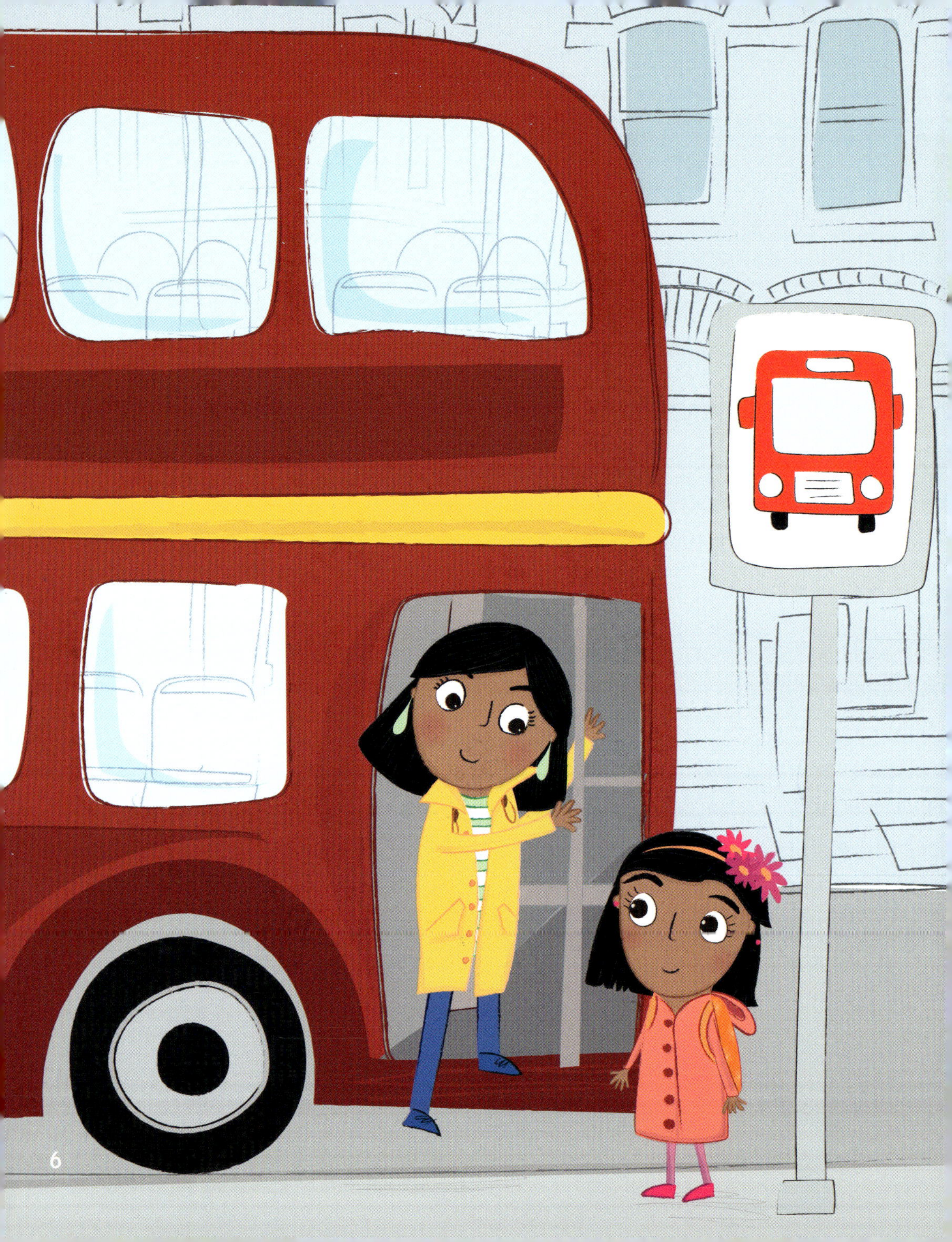

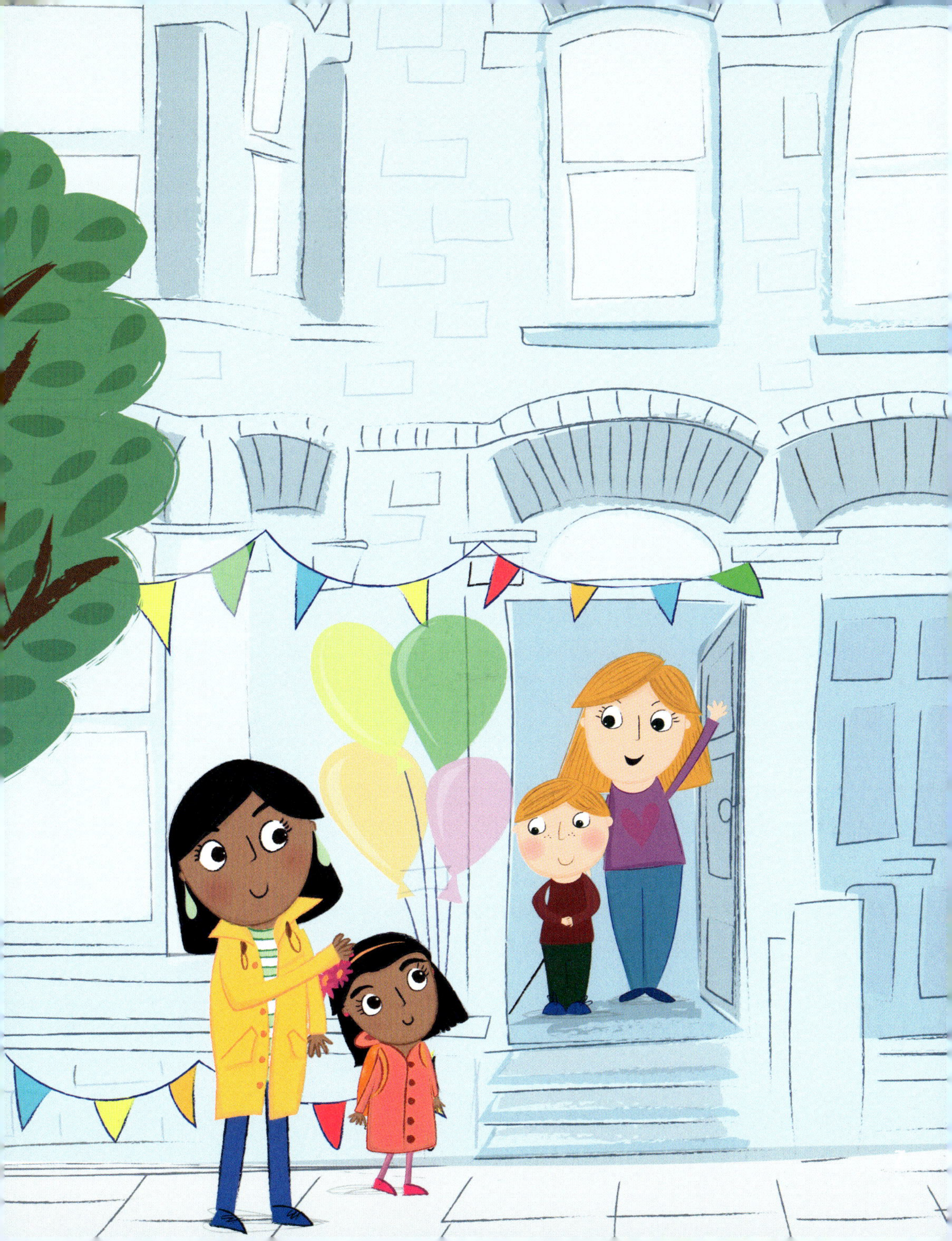

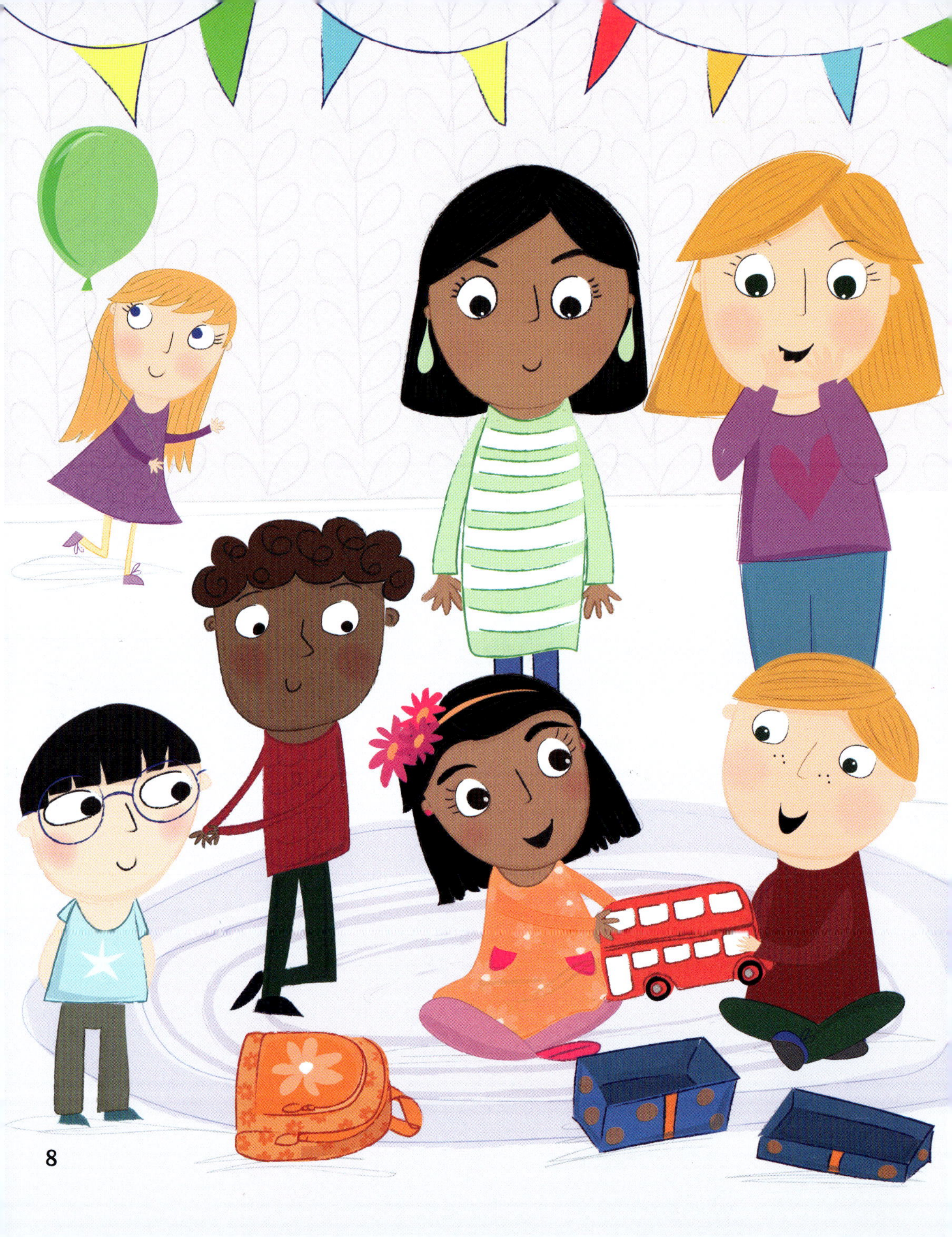